Contents

Abby has one balloon.

We Can Count!

Winston Scott

INFOMAX COMMON CORE READERS

Rosen Classroom™

New York

Published in 2013 by The Rosen Publishing Group, Inc.
29 East 21st Street, New York, NY 10010

Book Design: Michael J. Flynn

Photo Credits: Cover Africa Studio/Shutterstock.com; p. 5 Layland Masuda/Shutterstock.com; pp. 7, 15 Apollofoto/Shutterstock.com; p. 9 © iStockphoto.com/Ashok Rodrigues; p. 11 popovich_vl/Shutterstock.com; p. 13 SergiyN/Shutterstock.com.

ISBN: 978-1-4488-8887-0
6-pack ISBN: 978-1-4488-8888-7

Manufactured in the United States of America

CPSIA Compliance Information: Batch #WS12RC: For further information contact Rosen Publishing, New York, New York at 1-800-237-9932.

Word Count: 24

Ethan has two balloons.

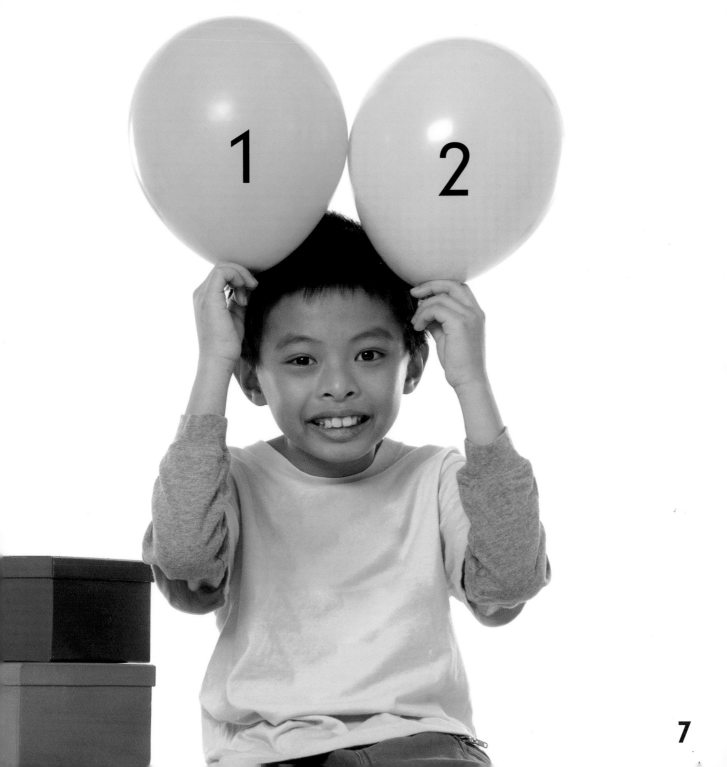

Jenna has three balloons.

Kate has four balloons.

Charlie has five balloons.

1

2

3

4

5

We have six balloons.

Words to Know

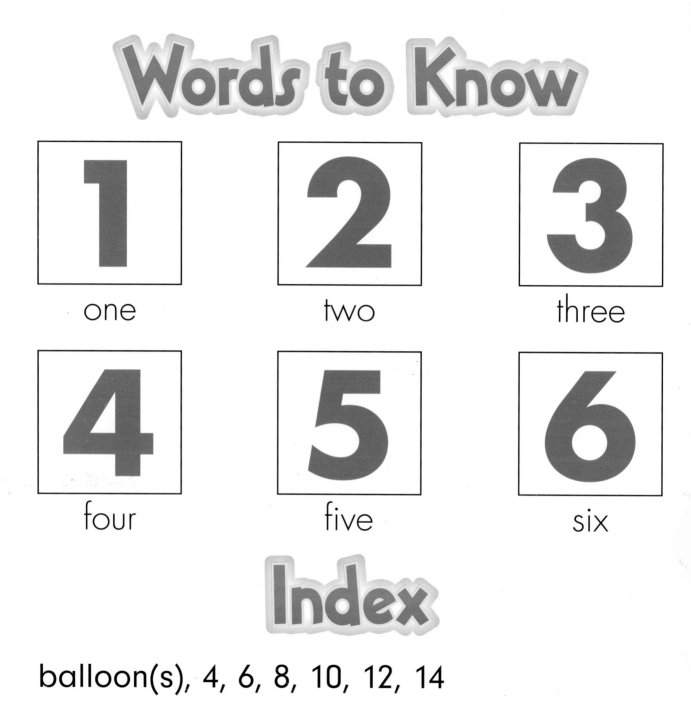

1 one

2 two

3 three

4 four

5 five

6 six

Index